Business Card Origami

Nick Robinson

imagine!
Publishing

Business Card Origami

Nick Robinson

imagine!
Publishing

An Imagine Book
Published by Charlesbridge
85 Main Street, Watertown, MA 02472
(617) 926-0329
www.charlesbridge.com

Printed in China, April 2014.

The publisher does not have any control over and does not assume any responsibility
for author or third-party websites or their content.

ISBN 978-1-62354-019-7

2 4 6 8 10 9 7 5 3 1

For information about custom editions, special sales, and premium and corporate
purchases, please contact Charlesbridge Publishing at specialsales@charlesbridge.com.

Dedication

The book is dedicated to my beautiful wife, Alison, my children, Nick and Daisy, plus the cats, Matilda and Rhubarb.

Author's Note

Many folders have created business card models, but applying generic origami techniques isn't difficult, so it's tricky to say who created a given model first. However, credit must go to Valerie Vann, Jennifer Campbell, and Jeannine Mosely, who have done much work in this area. Many thanks to Malachi Brown for his expertise and willingness to help with this project.

Sail Away, Mini Hoop, Stuffed Shirt, and Bottle Cap are based on traditional origami designs. Cubicle of Doom is based on work by Paul Jackson, Desk Dog, on work by John Smith. Toy Froggy and Jabber Jaws are traditional business card designs. Business Card Death Star was created by Wayne Brown. All other designs were discovered and created independently by the author. All the information on the cards is fictitious!

The author's website is www.origami.me.uk.
Malachi Brown's site is www.spencerandbrown.com/mbb/origami

Contents

Introduction

*Y*ou would think that by this point in the 21st century, we'd be done with paper business cards already. However, according to www.statisticbrain.com, approximately 10 billion business cards are printed in the United States every year. We hand them out and get them at conventions and conferences and in meetings and bars. We use them to write notes we promptly lose and to pick lunch out of our teeth. We give them to friends, collect them from colleagues, and more often than not, toss them in the trash as soon as possible. In fact, of those 10 billion cards we pass around every year, 8.8 billion of them are on their way to the landfill (or recycling center) within a week. But life doesn't have to be like that. You can make a difference with the business cards you collect or have stored, unused, in the bottom drawer of your desk. How? Create awesome origami projects with them. Sure, you've tried paper clip sculptures and stop-motion sticky note movies, but there's something timeless and precious about using your hands to turn a vendor's business card into a dog or a tiny basketball hoop. All you have to do is follow the fully illustrated, step-by-step instructions in this awesome book. The twenty projects, created by me and some of my origami expert friends, are simple to create, great fun for around the office, and perhaps, most excitingly, time consuming. Whether you're taking a five-minute break between meetings or a five-hour mini vacation, these projects will keep you busy.

Business Card Folding Basics

- The projects in this book use standard business cards that are 2 x 3.5 inches.

- Unlike traditional origami paper, business cards are thick. This prevents us from making complex origami-style models, but there is still much that can be done.

- The key skill to develop is creating neat, sharp creases. Some types of card allow this, while others tend to "crumple" rather than crease, which will leave your edges not as neat as you might wish. For great creases, find a ballpoint pen that has run out of ink, and, along with a small ruler, use it to "draw" the creases. This process (known as "scoring") creates a perfect folding crease and is well worth the extra time it may take.

Origami Folding Basics

The how-to illustrations in this book all use the same simple visual cues to show you what to do. Refer to these pages if you get confused. When you see color, that means the business card's design is facing up. If it's white, the card is face down.

VALLEY FOLD

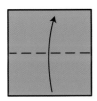 

VALLEY FOLD AND UNFOLD

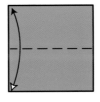 

MOUNTAIN FOLD

 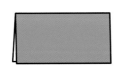

REPEAT THE STEP

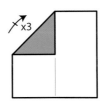

TURN THE CARD OVER

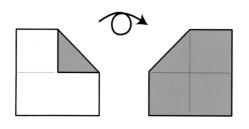

ROTATE THE CARD

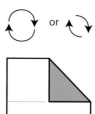 or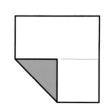

PUSH IN

 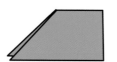

FOLD TO DOTTED LINE

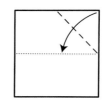 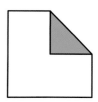

King or Queen for a Day

"IT'S GOOD TO BE THE KING," SAYS MEL BROOKS' LOUIS XVI IN *HISTORY OF THE WORLD, PART 1.* PERHAPS THIS CROWN, MADE UP OF FOUR OF YOUR BOSS'S BUSINESS CARDS, WILL MAKE YOU FEEL A TAD BIT BETTER ABOUT THE FACT THAT YOU ARE NOT THE OFFICE MONARCH.

This design uses four cards, and once you get the hang of it, try making it with even more. Experiment with how far you slide them into each other to get a firm lock.

1. A diagonal crease is quite hard to fold, so use a blunt point (such as an empty ballpoint pen) and a ruler to "draw" a neat crease.

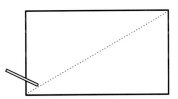

2. Fold on the diagonal.

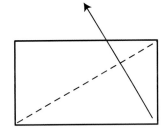

3. The unit is complete (yes!). Make three more.

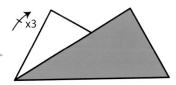

4. Slide the left unit into the right unit until the upper corners meet.

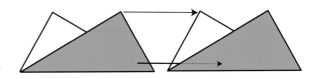

5. Gently curl the cards so they form a "C" shape.

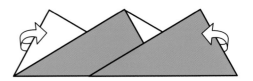

6. Join the other two units in the same way.

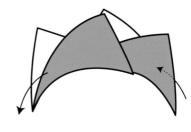

7. Here it is, the completed crown.

Last Day Box

AS YOU DREAM YOUR DAY AWAY, PRETEND THIS BOX IS A TINY FACSIMILE OF THE ONE THAT WILL ONE DAY CONTAIN THE CONTENTS OF YOUR DESK. NO, OF COURSE YOU WEREN'T FIRED! COME ON! TRY TO KEEP THOSE DAYDREAMS POSITIVE.

This design can be varied to produce boxes of different proportions. You'll need four cards for this project.

1. With the inner side of a business card facing upwards, fold the lower edge to lie on the left edge.

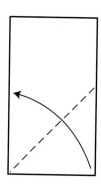

2. Fold the right vertical edge to the left edge. Crease and unfold.

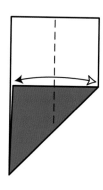

3. Fold the lower corner to the inner colored corner. Crease and unfold.

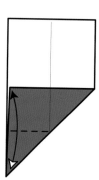

4. Fold the upper edge to lie on the most recent crease.

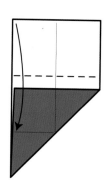

5. Reinforce these valley folds so that the faces are at right angles.

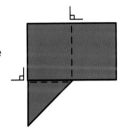

6. Here is a completed unit. Now, make three more.

7. Turn two units over and arrange as shown in the illustration. (The upper flap of the right unit slides into the top pocket of the unit on the left. The lower flap on the left simply goes behind the matching flap on the right.)

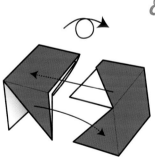

8. Here are the two units joined. Rotate the model counterclockwise.

9. Slide a third unit in the same way as in step 7.

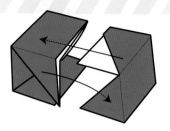

10. Here are the three units joined together. Rotate the model counterclockwise.

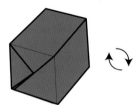

11. Join the final unit in the same way as the others. It may help to loosen all the units, insert the fourth, and then tighten them up.

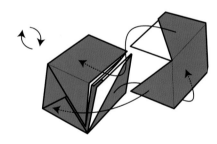

12. Here are the four units joined. Stand the model up: here is your completed box.

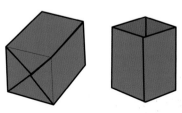

Things Are Pointing Up

SALES PROJECTIONS HAVE YOU DOWN? STOCK PRICES IN THE TOILET? PLACE THIS ARROW OVER YOUR REPORTS IN AN UPWARD POSITION TO SHOW YOUR HOPELESS OPTIMISM.

rder

This is a great beginner's project that only uses one business card.

1. Fold a short edge to a long edge. Crease and unfold.

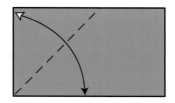

2. Repeat in the opposite direction.

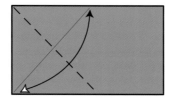

3. Fold upper and lower edges to the center, but only crease on the right side of the card.

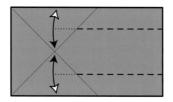

4. Turn the card over. Fold the left edge to the ends of the creases.

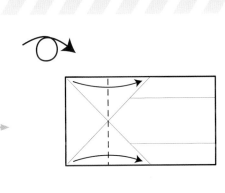

5. This is the result.

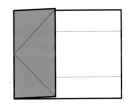

6. Turn the card over. Fold the left corners in on existing creases.

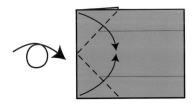

7. Refold the creases made in step 3. The crease extends under the triangular flaps.

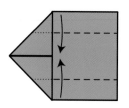

8. Turn the card over for the finished arrow.

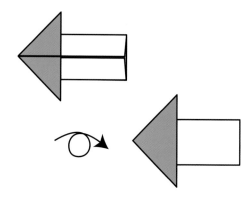

Cubicle of Doom

CREATE HUNDREDS OF THESE CUBES TO CLOSE OFF THE SPACE WHERE YOUR FOURTH WALL SHOULD BE. WHOEVER THOUGHT CUBICLES WERE A GOOD IDEA SHOULD HAVE ONE WALL OF THEIR HOUSE DEMOLISHED.

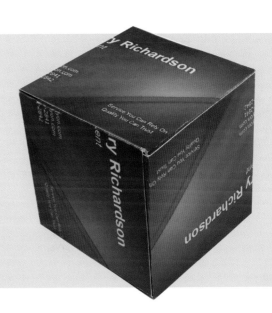

You'll need six business cards—one for each side of the cube. The overlapping short flaps created in step 3 create the tension that holds the units together.

1. Overlap two business cards as shown in the illustration so the white flaps are approximately the same size. Fold the white flaps over the edge of the upper card and unfold.

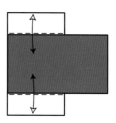

2. Turn the cards over, and arrange the layers in the same way and repeat step 1. Unfold the two cards and repeat with all the cards.

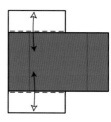

3. Open the flaps out at slightly less than 90 degrees and slide one short flap into the other card until the angled corners meet.

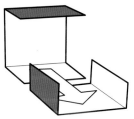

4. Slide a third card in to complete a corner.

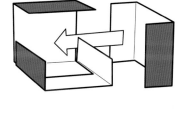

5. Add the fourth.

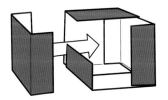

6. And the fifth.

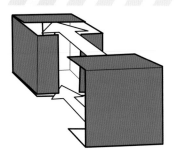

7. Finally, slide the last card into place and tighten all the corners.

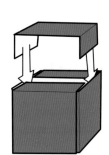

8. Voilà!

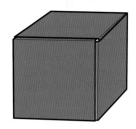

Forgot-Me-Nots

HE FORGOT YOUR ANNIVERSARY/YOUR BIRTHDAY/VALENTINE'S DAY AGAIN?! MAKE ONE OR MORE OF THESE FLOWERS FOR YOURSELF WHILE COMPOSING YOUR BREAK-UP SPEECH.

You will need four business cards for one flower.

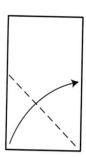

1. Fold the lower edge of one business card to the right edge.

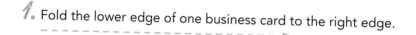

2. Fold the upper, white edge to the colored edge, and then unfold.

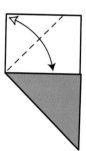

3. Turn the business card over. Fold the existing crease over to this side.

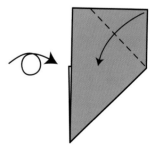

4. Fold the right corner to the left. Crease and unfold. Turn the paper over. This is one finished unit. Now, make three more.

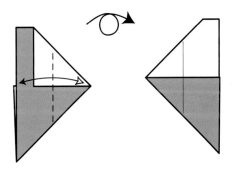

5. Arrange two units as shown in the illustration and slide one into the other.

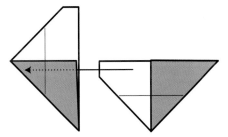

6. Refold this mountain crease to add it to the inner unit, and then separate the units. Repeat this process with every card.

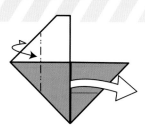

7. Slide the four units into each other. This is the result.

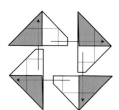

8. Now, turn the model over. Fold down the inner right flap.

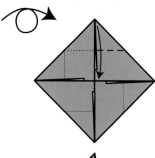

9. Now, fold the upper left flap.

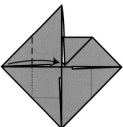

10. And the lower left flap.

-------- ➤

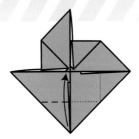

11. And the lower right flap!

-------- ➤

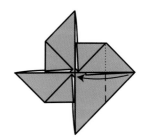

12. Turn the model over, and let the "petals" rise up naturally.

-------- ➤

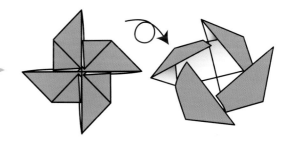

Jet Setter

WITH THIS PROJECT,
YOUR BUSINESS CARD
WILL TAKE YOUR NAME
TO NEW HEIGHTS . . .
LITERALLY.

The best way to get this tiny plane off the ground is to throw it high in the air. Fold the wings at slightly different angles until your flyer is achieving maximum altitude.

1. Fold the business card in half from side to side. Crease and unfold.

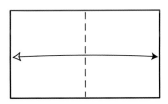

2. Fold each half of the lower edge to the vertical center.

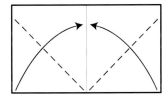

3. Fold the lower corner to the inner colored corners. Crease and unfold.

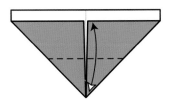

4. Fold the same corner to the newest crease.

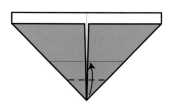

5. Refold the earlier crease.

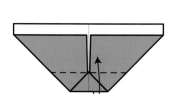

6. Fold the right half of the card behind. Rotate the paper.

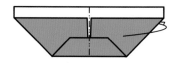

7. Fold a wing down to lie on the lower edge.

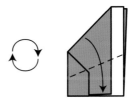

8. Repeat step 7.

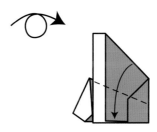

9. You're ready for lift off.

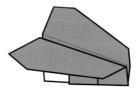

Heart Attack

MAKE A HEART TO REMIND YOURSELF THAT YOUR SUPER SEDENTARY JOB IS STEALING YEARS OFF YOUR LIFE. THAT IS UNLESS YOU HAVE A STATIONARY BIKE UNDER YOUR DESK.

You can fold one of these hearts in under 30 seconds once you get the hang of it.

1. Fold a business card in half, short edge to short edge. Crease and unfold.

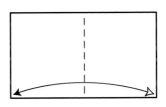

2. Fold half of the lower edge to lie on the (imaginary) dotted line.

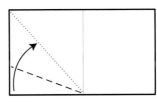

3. Fold the top left corner, creating a small triangle.

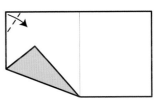

4. Fold the model in half from left to right.

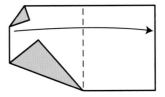

5. Fold over and unfold the white flaps.

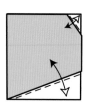

6. Unfold the upper layer.

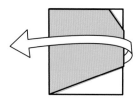

7. Fold over on the creases made in step 5.

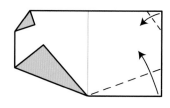

8. The folds are now symmetrical.
   Fold in half to the right.

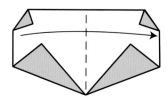

9. Fold over the corner, crease firmly, and then unfold.

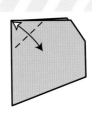

10. Push the corner inside the model.

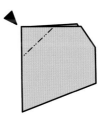

11. Open out a layer from underneath.

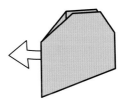

12. Your heart is complete.

Jabber Jaws

WITH ONE CREASE AND A FEW FOLDS, YOU CAN QUICKLY TURN A USELESS BUSINESS CARD INTO A MINI PUPPET YOU CAN USE DURING THE COMPANY-WIDE MEETING TO MIMIC THE GUY IN MARKETING WHO WON'T SHUT UP.

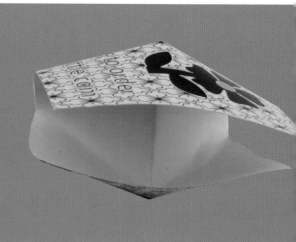

1. Lift up one end of a business card and bend it into the shape of a letter "C."

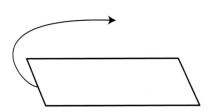

2. Hold the sides with a finger and thumb of one hand, and then use a finger from the other hand to press gently into the center. Make just a small crease. The dotted lines show where a soft crease is formed.

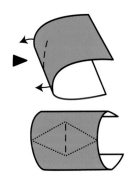

3. Once the vertical crease is in place, you can use one hand to gently press the sides together to operate the jaws.

Octahedron

THIS DESIGN HAS EIGHT FACES—ALL EQUILATERAL TRIANGLES. TELL YOUR COWORKERS THIS SHAPE IS ONE OF THE PLATONIC SOLIDS, AND YOU MAY FIND ALL YOUR POTENTIAL ROMANTIC RELATIONSHIPS SUDDENLY SOLIDLY PLATONIC.

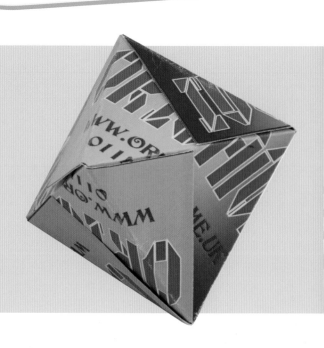

1. Fold a business card from the bottom right to the top left. Crease and unfold.

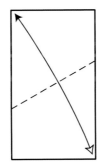

2. Fold the left edge that lies below the crease over to meet the crease, and then unfold.

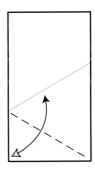

3. This is the result. Rotate the paper 180 degrees.

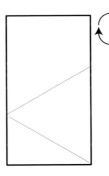

4. Repeat step 2.

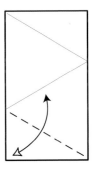

5. Here's a complete unit. Make three more.

6. Arrange two units like this. Overlap the small flaps.

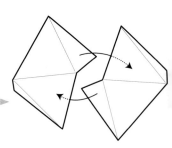

7. This is the result.

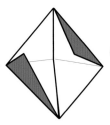

8. Place a third unit as shown. Overlap a single flap from two units.

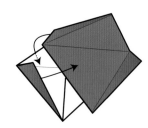

9. The final unit slides into the gap, with four flaps overlapping. Tighten all units for the finished model.

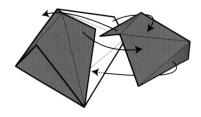

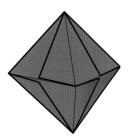

Sail Away

THINK OF THIS PROJECT AS A REALITY-BUILDING EXERCISE. YOU WORK FOR THE MAN AND ALWAYS WILL. SO, IMAGINE YOUR DREAMS OF FAME AND SUCCESS SAIL AWAY AS YOU "BUILD" THIS LITTLE BOAT.

If you place a small weight inside the boat, it will actually float!

1. Place the outer side upwards, and fold the card in half upwards.

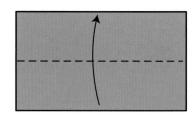

2. Fold a single layer from the top edge to the lower edge.

3. This is the result. Turn the card over.

4. Fold the top edge to the lower edge. Crease and unfold.

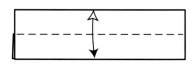

5. Fold all the corners into the horizontal crease.

6. Fold the model in half.

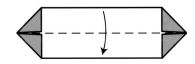

7. Hold the ends circled in the illustration and gently press from underneath to open and shape the boat.

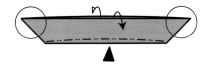

Snakes on a Desk

TIRED OF MAKING RUBBER-BAND BALLS AND PAPER CLIP CHAINS? HERE'S THE LATEST OFFICE SUPPLY TIME WASTER. YOUR SNAKE'S LENGTH DEPENDS ON HOW MANY BUSINESS CARDS YOU HAVE ON HAND AND HOW CLOSE YOUR BOSS HAPPENS TO BE.

You will need at least two business cards for this project, although you can extend the length of your snake as far as you want by using the technique shown in steps 3 through 5. You can also try to make the body more rounded and lifelike by pressing down on the top of the back.

1. Fold one business card in half, long edge to long edge. Crease and unfold.

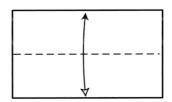

2. Fold the long edges to the center. Crease and unfold.

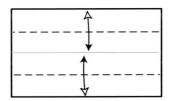

3. Fold over a short strip on the right.

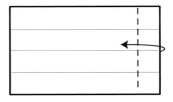

4. Fold another card in the same way and tuck it under the flap, colored side upward.

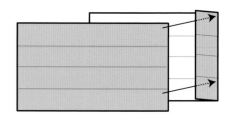

5. Fold the flap to the right along the raw edge.

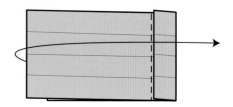

6. Fold the right corners to the center.

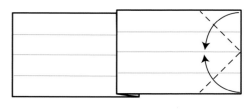

7. Fold the long edges to the center.

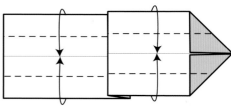

8. Fold the left corners and the right edges to the center.

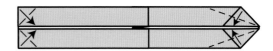

9. Make a pleat on the left.

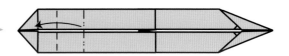

10. Fold the model in half, downward.

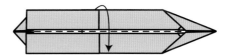

11. Hold the model at the circles, and then carefully but firmly pull the head upward and squeeze flat when it is in the right position.

12. Curl the tail.

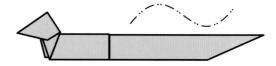

13. You're done!

Toy Froggy

TIRED OF PLOTTING
YOUR REVENGE ON JUST
ABOUT EVERYONE FROM
THE MAILROOM GUY TO
THE CEO? CREATE THIS
BRILLIANT TOY THAT WILL
JUMP RIGHT ACROSS
YOUR DESK. HOURS OF
FUN AWAIT.

The trick to getting your toy froggy to jump is to not press so hard that the curved paper flattens.

1. Fold the lower edge of a business card to the right edge. Crease and unfold.

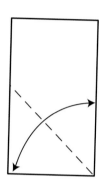

2. Repeat the fold in the other direction.

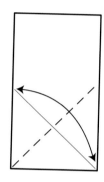

3. Turn the business card over and then fold the lower edge to the ends of the creases. Unfold.

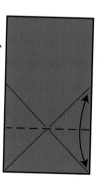

4. Turn the business card over, and collapse the paper upwards using the creases shown.

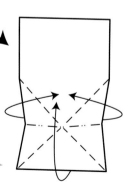

5. Fold the two small points to the lower corner.

------------->

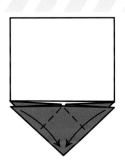

6. Rotate the project to the position shown in the illustration. Fold the upper and lower edges to the horizontal center.

------------->

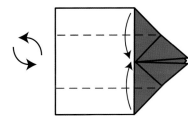

7. Fold the right end of the paper into a gentle "S" curve. Press the paper down slightly, and then flick your finger backwards.

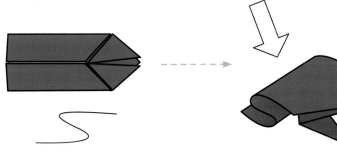

THIS PROJECT HONORS ANYONE WHO COMES OFF AS POMPOUS, SELF-SATISFIED, INFLEXIBLE, STIFF, USELESS, OR STUPID—A.K.A. ANYONE FROM CORPORATE.

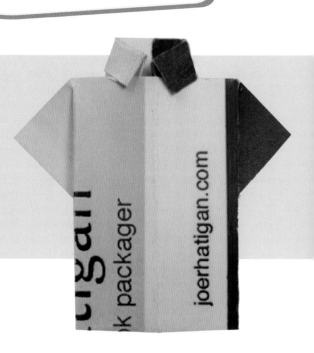

This is a great way to display your business card.

1. Fold a business card in half from side to side. Crease and unfold.

– ➤

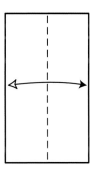

2. Fold the outer edges to the vertical crease.

– ➤

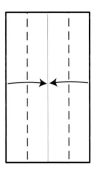

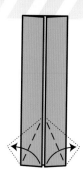

3. Fold both lower corners out to match the dotted lines.

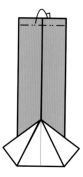

4. At the top, fold a tiny flap behind.

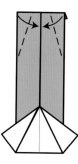

5. Fold the top corners inward so they meet just below the upper edge.

6. Fold the lower half upward and tuck under the "collar."

- ➤

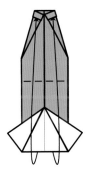

7. You're done.

- ➤

Desk Dog

THIS DOG'S HEAD WILL FOLLOW YOU AROUND THE ROOM AND IS REPUTED TO WOBBLE GENTLY WHEN THE SPIRIT OF YOUR YOUNGER, MORE AMBITIOUS SELF ENTERS YOUR CUBICLE.

You'll need two business cards for this project. Use two of the same card if you want a purebred. Mix and match if you want a mutt.

BODY

1. Fold the card for the body in half from side to side. Crease and unfold.

- ➔

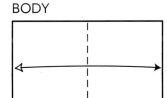

2. Fold the outer edges to the top edge. Crease and unfold where shown.

- ➔

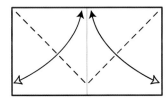

3. Fold up a short strip at the bottom. (The crease passes through the intersection of the previous creases.)

- ➔

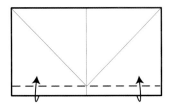

4. Fold in half from right to left.

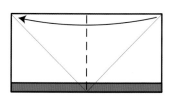

5. Fold the bottom right corner up to the top left corner.

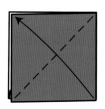

6. Rotate the card counterclockwise. The body is complete.

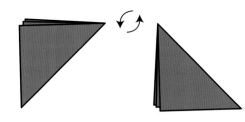

HEAD

7. Grab another card and fold it in half from side to side. Crease and unfold.

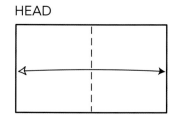

8. Fold the lower edges to the vertical center.

- ->

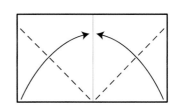

9. Fold a small corner underneath.

- ->

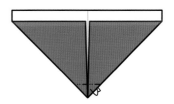

10. Fold in half from left to right.

- ->

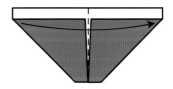

11. Fold a flap down.

- ->

12. Fold the same flap back to the right so it matches the dotted line.

13. Repeat steps 11 and 12 on the other side.

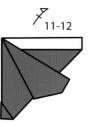

14. Rotate the card. Push the top corner inwards.

15. This is the view from the rear.

16. Balance the head onto the body.

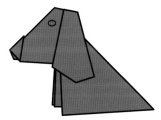

Mini Hoop

AND WHO SAID YOU COULDN'T DUNK . . .

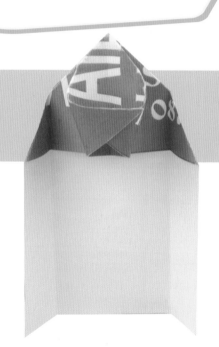

Only one business card needed here. The idea is to crumple up a tiny sheet of paper to form a basketball, and then practice your three-point shot. You can make a larger hoop using a piece of copy paper.

1. Fold the short edge of a business card to a long edge. Crease and unfold.

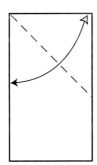

2. Repeat in the opposite direction.

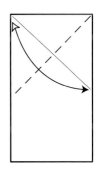

3. Turn the card over. Fold the top edge to the ends of the creases. Crease and unfold.

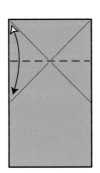

4. Turn the card over. Collapse the top of the card down using the creases.

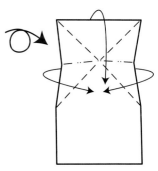

5. Fold the sides to the center, lifting the top layers out of the way. Crease and unfold.

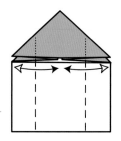

6. Curl the left flap over to the right.

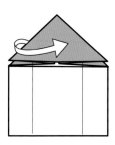

7. Do the same on the right, tucking one flap between layers of the other to form the hoop.

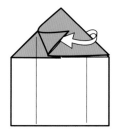

8. Fold the sides forward at 90-degree angles so the model will stand.

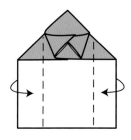

9. There's nothing holding you back now!

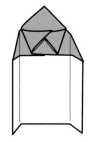

Frog Face

SOMEONE PARK IN YOUR SPOT THIS MORNING? LEAVE THIS LITTLE GUY ON THE WINDSHIELD ALONG WITH THIS NOTE: FROG PARKING ONLY . . . ALL OTHERS WILL BE TOAD. HOP TO IT!

One card is all you need for this ribbeting project.

1. Fold a business card in half, short edge to short edge. Crease and unfold.

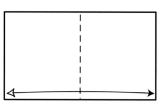

2. Fold the card in half long edge to long edge. Crease and unfold.

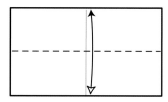

3. Fold the left edge to the center. Repeat on the right, but then unfold this side.

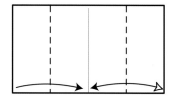

4. This is the result.

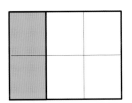

5. Turn the card over. Fold the left-hand corners in on the creases that run from the center of the left edge to the end of the vertical edge underneath. The edges will not line up with the vertical crease.

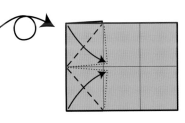

6. On the right, crease from the central intersection to the corners. Note that the edges should not line up. Turn the card over.

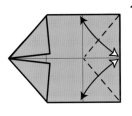

7. Rotate the card to this position. Fold the upper edge to the center.

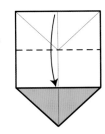

8. Fold two corners in for the eyes. The exact size isn't important.

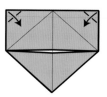

9. This is the result.

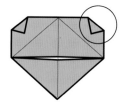

10. Lift one triangular eye flap up and partially squash it open, lifting the original edge up. Repeat with the other flap.

11. This is the result.

12. Hold the sides, press together, and use the creases shown to open the mouth.

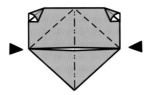

13. Meet your new frog face.

Bottle Cap

USE THIS CAP TO IDENTIFY YOUR BOTTLES IN THE FRIDGE. YOUR AFTER-LUNCH DIET COKE IS NOW SAFE.

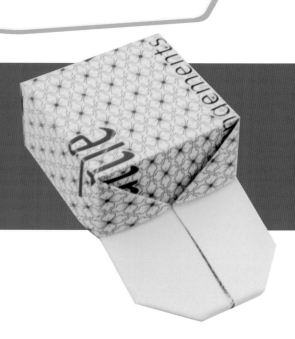

1. Fold the lower edge of a business card to the right edge, making a tiny pinch where shown. Unfold.

2. Fold the lower edge to the pinch. Crease and unfold.

3. Fold the lower edge to the new crease. Crease and unfold.

4. Turn the card over. Fold so that the bottom crease lines up with the left edge. Crease and unfold.

5. Repeat on the right side.

6. Turn the card over and rotate 180 degrees. Fold the card up to the top crease line and then unfold.

7. Fold the long edges to the center. Crease and unfold.

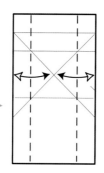

8. Use these new crease lines to lift the top end up as shown in the illustration.

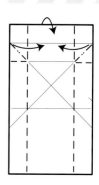

9. Fold the colored flap inside the model.

10. This is the result. Turn the card over.

11. Fold the flap down, bringing the sides together in the center, forming the bill.

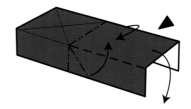

12. Fold the bill up as shown in the illustration.

13. Fold the corners inside the bill.

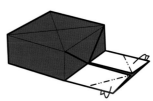

14. Fold the tip inside the bill.

15. Your cap is ready.

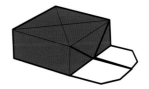

The Time Waster

THIS GEOMETRIC SHAPE CAN BE SEEN AS A CUBE WITH EACH CORNER SLICED OFF TO FORM A TRIANGULAR "HOLE." AND YOU'LL BE IN A BIG HOLE WITH THE BOSS IF YOU'RE CAUGHT CONSTRUCTING THIS WITH YOUR CLIENTS' BUSINESS CARDS.

1. Fold a card in half, short edge to short edge. This is the template for the next step.

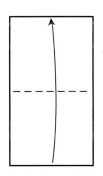

2. Insert a new card between the layers. Fold the left, white edge to lie along the folded card. Remove the folded card and set aside.

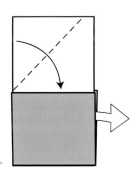

3. Fold the lower, white edge to lie along the colored edge. Unfold.

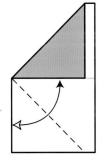

4. Make fold A, and then unfold the upper layer (B).

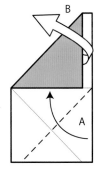

5. Crease and unfold (A), and then unfold the lower layer (B).

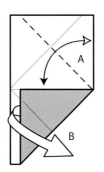

6. Turn the card over. Fold the edges at the center of each "X." Crease and unfold.

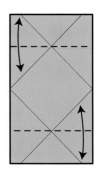

7. Turn the card over. Collapse the top edge downward using the creases.

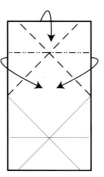

8. Repeat on the lower edge.

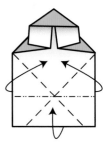

9. This is the result.

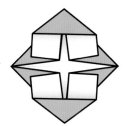

10. Open the creases out to this position. The unit is complete. Make five more.

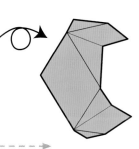

11. Tuck the outer flaps of one unit inside the next.

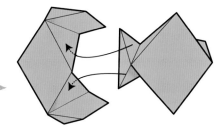

12. A third unit tucks inside one unit and outside the other.

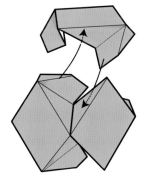

13. Here are three units together.

14. Rotate the project. Add a fourth unit in the same way.

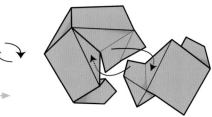

15. Add two more in the same way. You will need to slightly open the unit to insert the final one. Once all the pieces are together, tighten them.

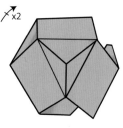

16. Here it is!

Business Card Death Star

YOU KNOW THAT GUY
THREE CUBICLES OVER
SINGING CHRISTMAS
CAROLS EVEN THOUGH
IT'S JULY? HIT HIM
WITH THIS.

You're only six business cards away from creating this awesome ninja weapon.

1. Fold the lower right corner of one card to the upper left corner.

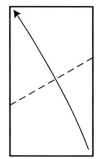

2. Fold corner to corner. Crease and unfold fully.

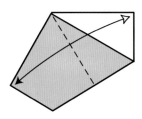

3. Fold two opposite corners to the center.

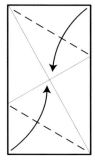

4. Fold in half from left to right.

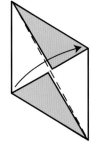

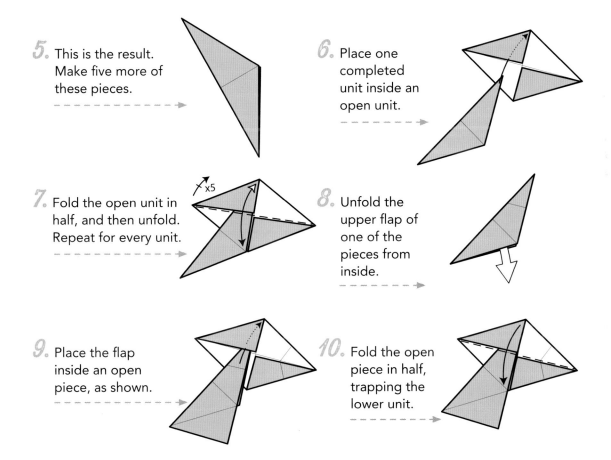

5. This is the result. Make five more of these pieces.

6. Place one completed unit inside an open unit.

7. Fold the open unit in half, and then unfold. Repeat for every unit.

×5

8. Unfold the upper flap of one of the pieces from inside.

9. Place the flap inside an open piece, as shown.

10. Fold the open piece in half, trapping the lower unit.

11. Slide the joined units into another open unit as shown.

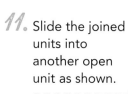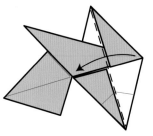

12. Add the fourth unit.

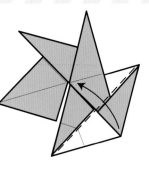

13. Add the fifth unit.

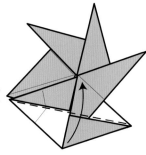

14. Add the sixth unit.

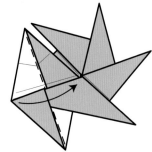

15. Fold the narrow flap to the center.

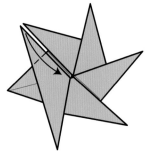

16. Wrap around (ease out) the unfolded flap from step 8 so it is on the top.

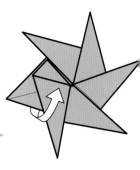

17. Fold this flap inside to complete the assembly.

-----------------→

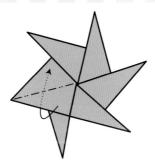

18. You may have to adjust the assembly a bit so it looks symmetrical.

-----------------→

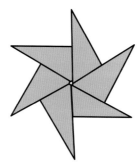

The Rising Star

LET THIS PROJECT REMIND YOU THAT ALL YOUR HARD WORK AT THE OFFICE WILL PAY OFF, AND YOU'LL EITHER BECOME THE RISING STAR YOU ALWAYS KNEW YOU'D BE, OR YOU'LL BECOME AN ORIGAMI EXPERT. EITHER WAY, GOOD LUCK!

You'll need six business cards for this project. The challenge here will come at step 7. Be patient and you'll get it.

1. Fold the lower left corner of a business card to the upper right corner.

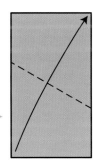

2. Fold corner to corner. Crease and unfold.

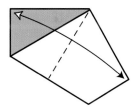

3. Unfold fully.

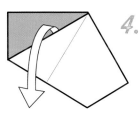

4. Turn the card over. Fold the outer edge to the crease, making the crease only where shown.

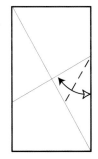

5. Fold the lower right corner to the end of the crease, again making the crease only where shown.

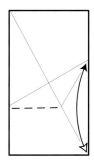

6. Turn the paper over.

7. Start forming the creases as shown in the illustration. Some of the card is trapped inside as you close the sides.

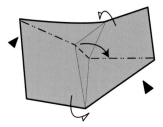

8. Fold the white edge on the right to the colored edge. Crease and unfold.

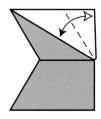

9. Make another five pieces like this.

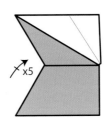

10. Arrange two units as shown and slide the yellow flap (second piece) under the green layer (first piece).

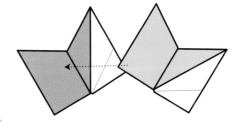

11. This is the result.

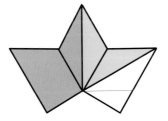

12. Turn the project over. Lock the units together by folding a flap into a pocket underneath.

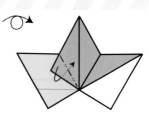

13. This is what it should look like at this point.

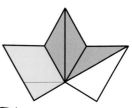

14. Turn the paper over. Slide in the next unit.

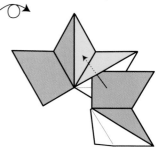

15. This is the result.

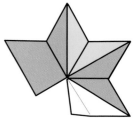

16. Turn the project over and lock as in step 12.

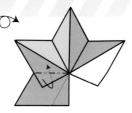

17. Repeat with the three remaining units.

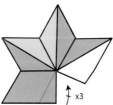

x3

18. Here is one side of the model.

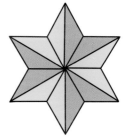

19. Turn the paper over. And here is the other!

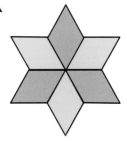

Index